The snagron

This book belongs to
Lancasterian Barrier Free
Partnership

Date of issue:

Please return when finished

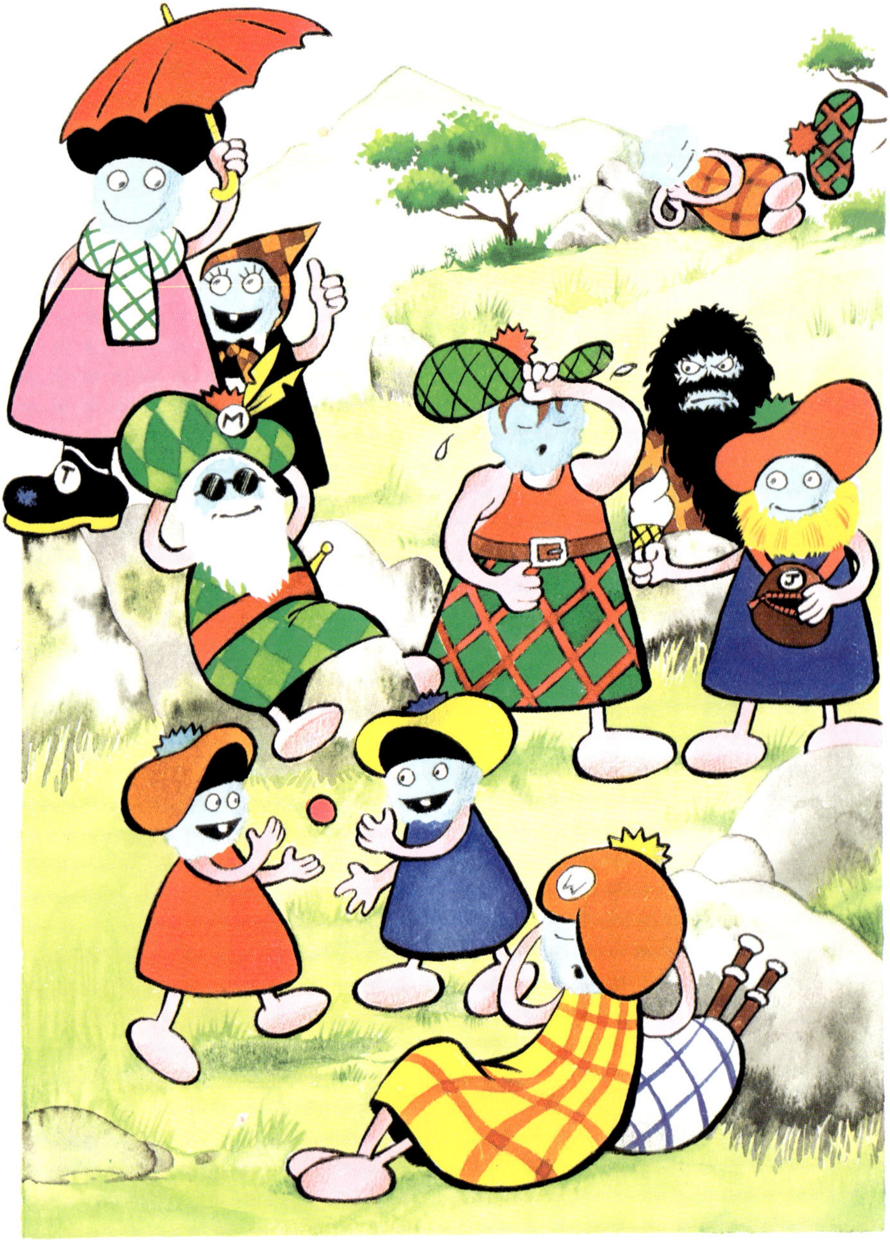

It was now two weeks after the clan had been on their visit to the Glen of Gloom.
It was a hot and sunny day in the Glen Macfuzz.
Everyone seemed to have forgotten about the monster which Ben had seen creeping out of the darkness of the cave.
The hot rays of the midday sun were beating down on the glen and there was not one cloud in the sky.
Every leaf on every tree was a fresh, green colour.
The River Mac was a deep, gleaming blue.
Everything in the glen was looking good.
The members of the clan were out in the glen.
They were as happy as larks.
They all felt as if they were on holiday.
They looked like a big, happy family.
Some of the clan were sitting under the trees.
Some of them felt drowsy because of the heat.
They intended to sleep the afternoon away.
Others were not sleepy at all.
They just sat together and chatted.

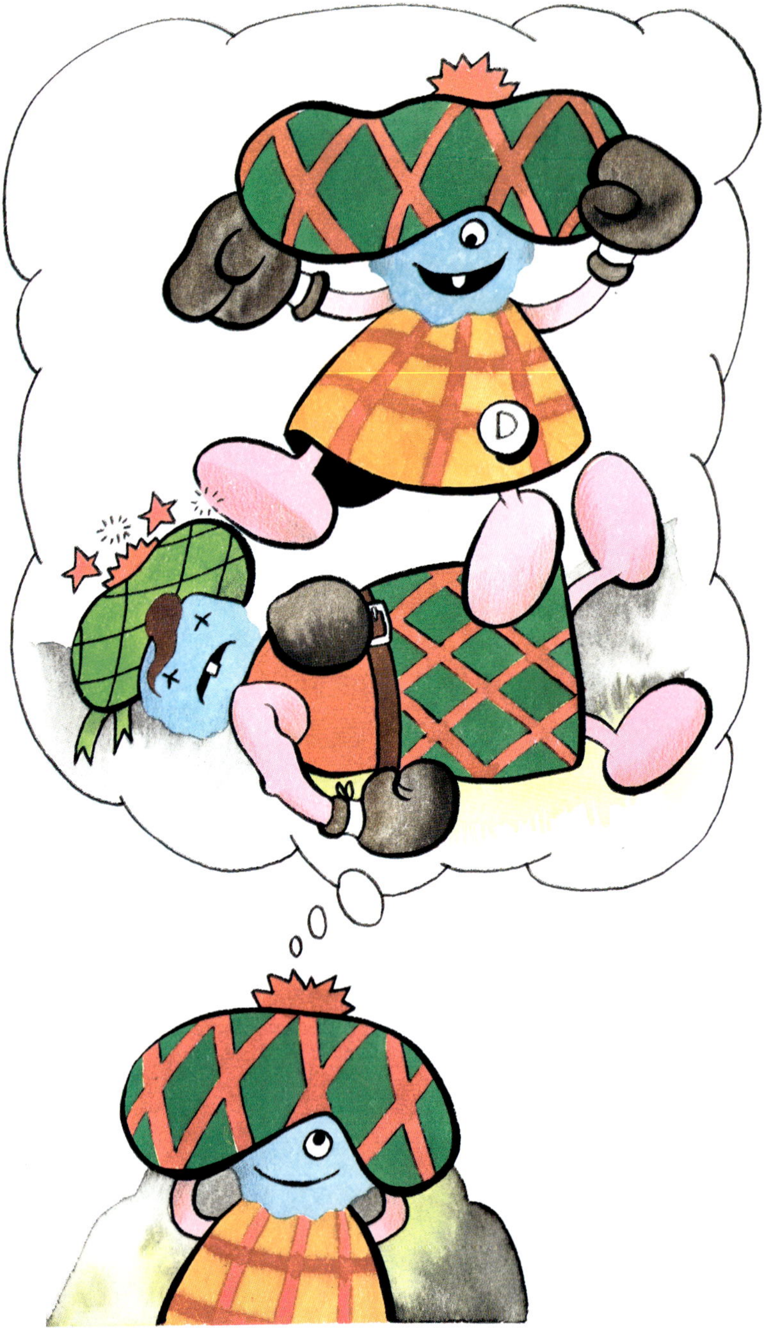
D

Little Don sat by himself.
He was day-dreaming.
His dream was that he was the biggest fuzzbuzz of all.
In his day-dream he had just beaten Big Ben in a boxing match!
He was grinning to himself, and dreaming that one day his wish would be granted.
Hilda had too much to do to think about sleeping or day-dreaming.
She was mixing up some cool orange drinks to give to the little ones.
She was going to treat them to a box full of apples and a tray full of cream buns too.
They would think that they were having a party!

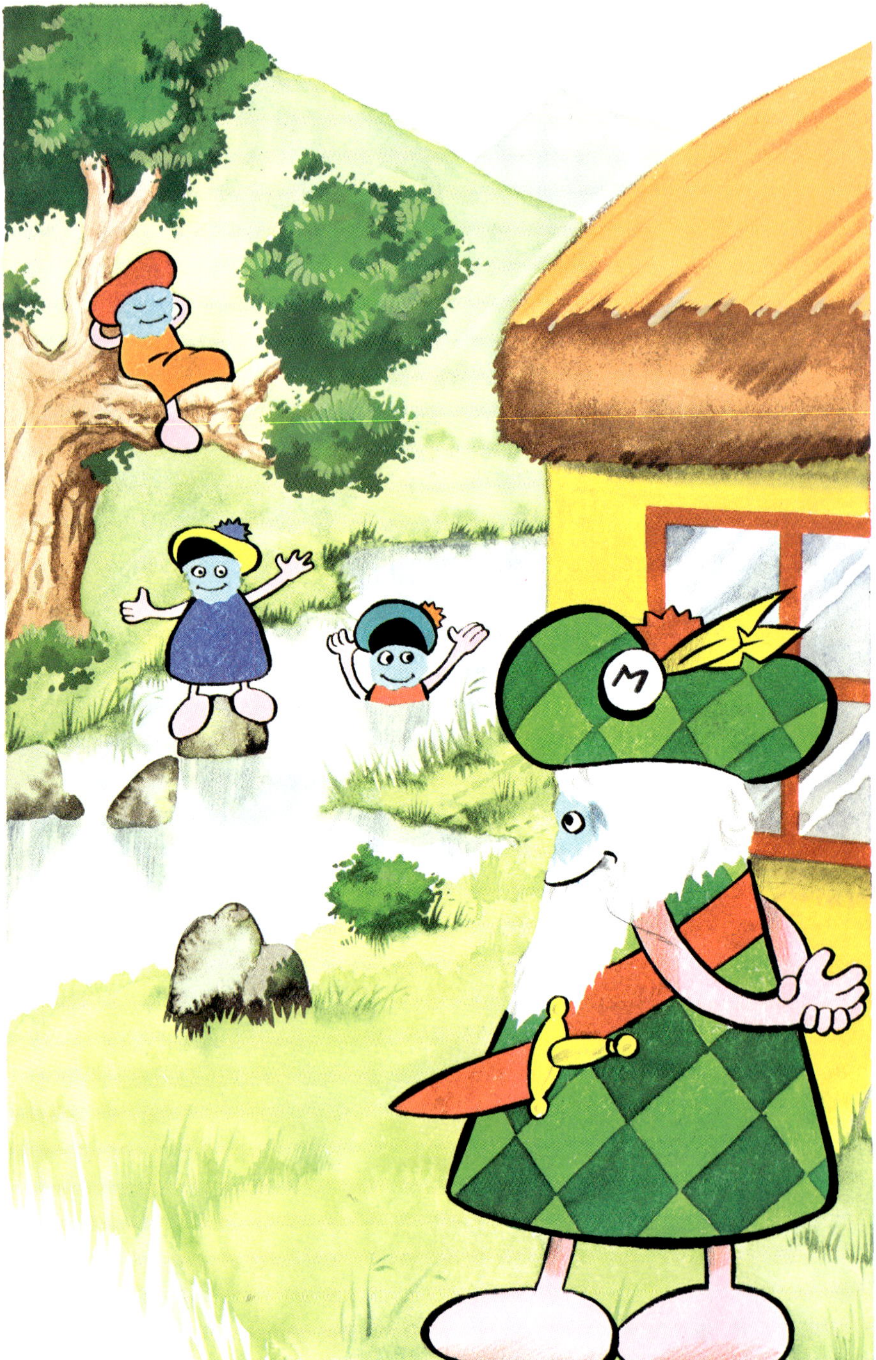
M

The little ones were playing down by the river.
They were having smashing fun.
They were larking about, screaming and shouting, and showering each other with sprays of water.
Macfuzz the buzz, who was the leader of the clan, stood by his croft and looked around.
He was glad to see that so many of his clan were looking happy and gay.
They were all having a good time.
But Macfuzz the buzz had not forgotten about the thing in the cave.
He had spent days thinking about it, and praying that the monster would not come looking for them.
But he didn't mean to stop the fun.
He was happy to see that today everyone was in a jolly mood.
He looked down towards the river bank, where the little ones were still clowning about.
At least they didn't think that the monster was coming to get them.
He took one more look around the glen, and then he went back into his house.

But Macfuzz the buzz had not looked as far as the top of the hills.
If he had, he would have been very upset.
The snagron was up there, peeping down at the clan.
She was partly hidden by a mound of green ferns which had sprouted up from the hill-top.
Her beady, blood-shot eyes were keenly inspecting the glen.

She had come out on a scouting trip and she was not very happy about what she had found. She could see that the clan were having a good time.
They must have stopped thinking about her. This made her feel very angry, very angry indeed.
Did they think that she would allow them to stray into her glen without paying for it?
   'Hiss!'
Her ugly head was swaying.
Her powerful tail was swishing.
Her sharp teeth were snapping.
Her long red tongue was darting in and out of her mouth.
Her eyes were mean and hard.
'You fools!' she hissed. 'I will soon put a stop to your fun.'
Thick jets of yellow mist came shooting from her nostrils.
This mist drifted around her like clouds of yellow steam.

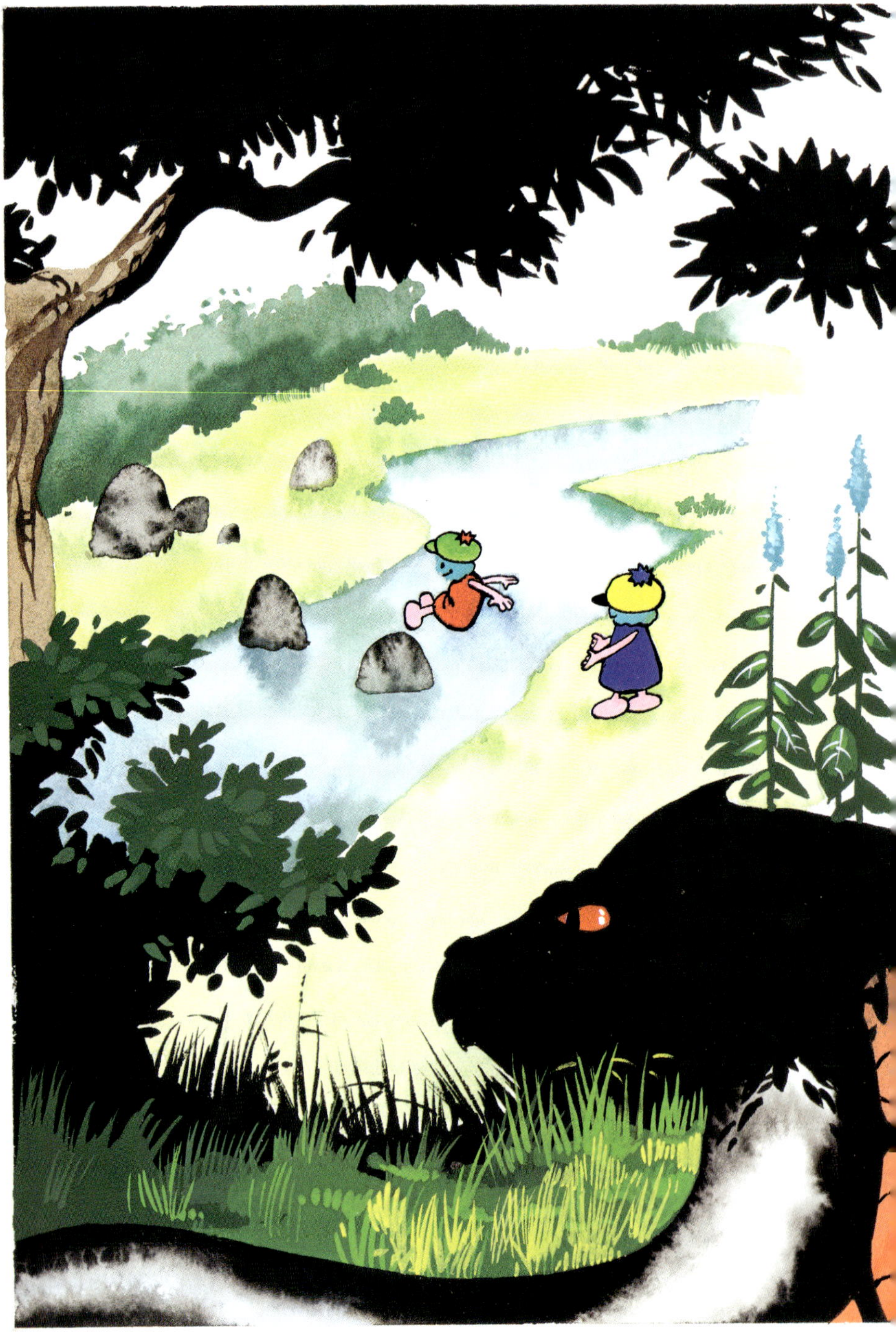

The snagron began to creep along the ground, keeping her body as flat as she possibly could. She intended to sneak down into the glen without anyone seeing her.
The yellow mist drifted downhill with her.
At last she came to a little wood.
She crept into the shelter of the trees, and then she stopped.
She would stay here for a bit, and keep a sharp look-out.
If she was very lucky, she would be able to waylay one of the clan and ask some questions.
Then, when she was ready, she would swoop into the attack!

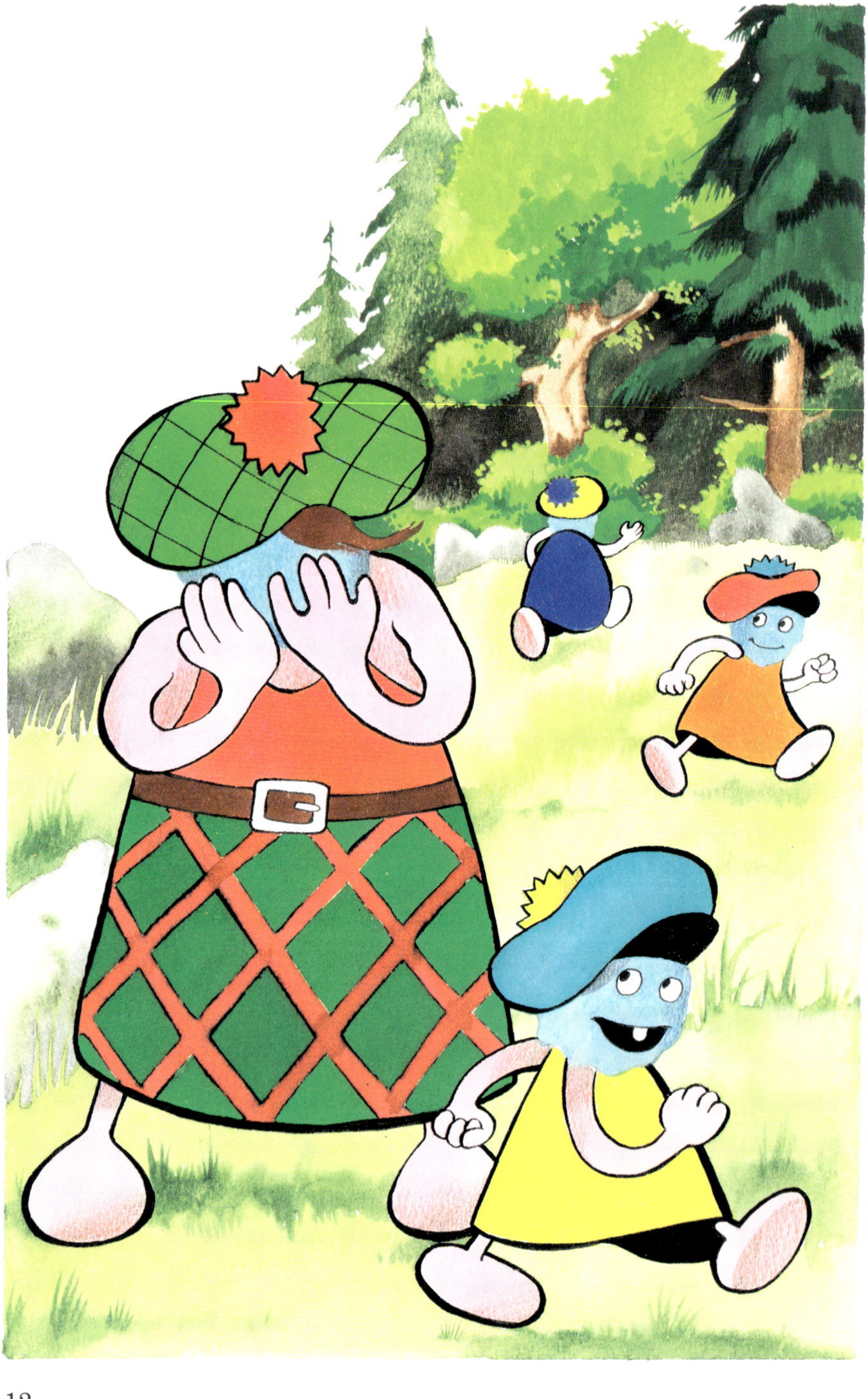

The little fuzzbuzzes were still down by the river.
Some of them were playing leap-frog.
The rest of them were playing hide-and-seek.
Big Ben was with them.
He was in a playful mood.
He shut his eyes and started to count.
All the little fuzzbuzzes darted off to hide somewhere.
Big Ben counted up to one hundred, then he stopped.
'Coming for you now!' he shouted. Then he began to look for them.
Before too long, he had found them all.
They were just getting ready to start again, when one of the little ones asked,
'Where's Freddy?'
Everyone looked around.
Little Freddy was missing.
He was nowhere to be seen.
'Come out, come out, wherever you are!' shouted Big Ben.
But there was no answer.
Ben shook his head.

14

'He must have gone back to his house for something to eat,' he said. 'Come on, let's play for a bit longer.'
But little Freddy had not gone back to his house.
As soon as Big Ben had started counting, he had gone zooming up the hill as fast as he could.
He ran up towards the woods.
Big Ben would never see him up there!
Before Ben had stopped counting, Freddy had darted into the trees.
Soon Freddy was straying into the deepest part of the wood.
But he had stopped running.
It was beginning to get darker, and everything felt creepy.
Strands of clammy, wet mist were creeping between the trees and along the ground.
Freddy felt a freezing shiver running up and down his back.

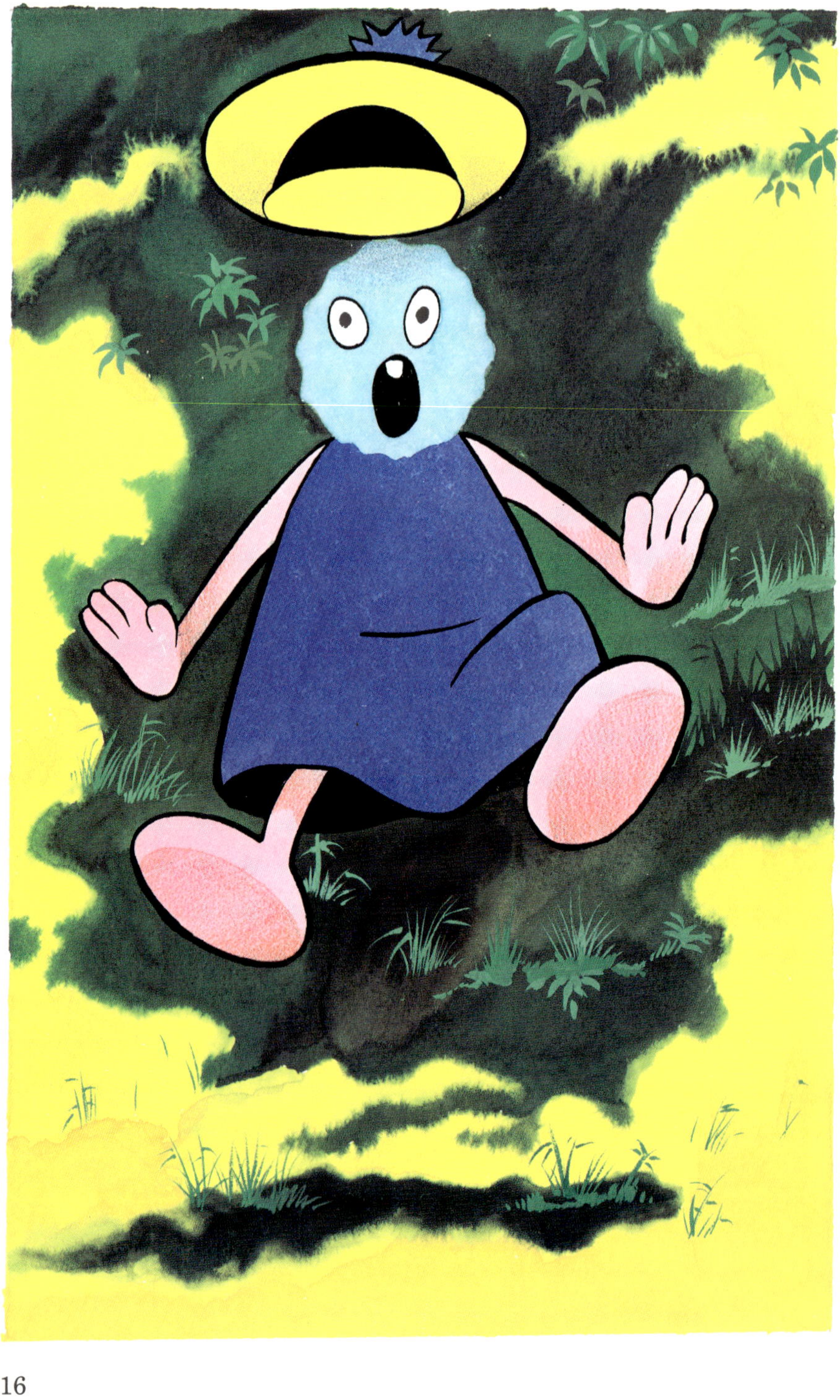

The yellow mist was streaming all around him.
His eyes were smarting and he could not see where he was going.
His head was ringing.
It was like drowning in a deep, yellow sea.
There was a horrid, foul smell.
Freddy wanted to be sick.
He stopped.
He had lost his way.
He knew that he would be better staying where he was, but something seemed to be leading him on.
A soft growling sound came out of the mist.
Freddy went towards it.
Suddenly, the thick mist parted.
With a gasp, Freddy took a step back.

Two blood-red eyes were scowling at him.
An ugly head, on the end of a long
arching neck, came towering out of the mist.
A long red tongue came streaking towards him.
The little fuzzbuzz stood rooted to the spot.
He could not run away.
'Have you come to see me, my little darling?'
hissed the snagron. 'Have you come to pay
me a visit? How sweet of you, my love. I'm
so glad that you could come.'

Freddy's feet were stuck to the ground.
His legs felt as wobbly as a jelly.
He wanted to run away, but he could not stop himself from looking into her two beady eyes.
His flesh was creeping.
He could not speak.
He wanted to scream as loudly as he could.
But it was no good.
He was spellbound by the snagron's sparkling eyes.
She had him in her power.
'Have you lost your tongue?' she hissed.
'Have you nothing to say for yourself? Come on, little one, you can speak to me.'
'Who are you?' asked Freddy.
'Who am I?' she hissed.
Her eyes began to glitter, and the red crest on the back of her neck stood out stiffly.
'I am the snagron, the powerful queen of the Glen of Gloom! You little fool, you should be bowing down before me!'

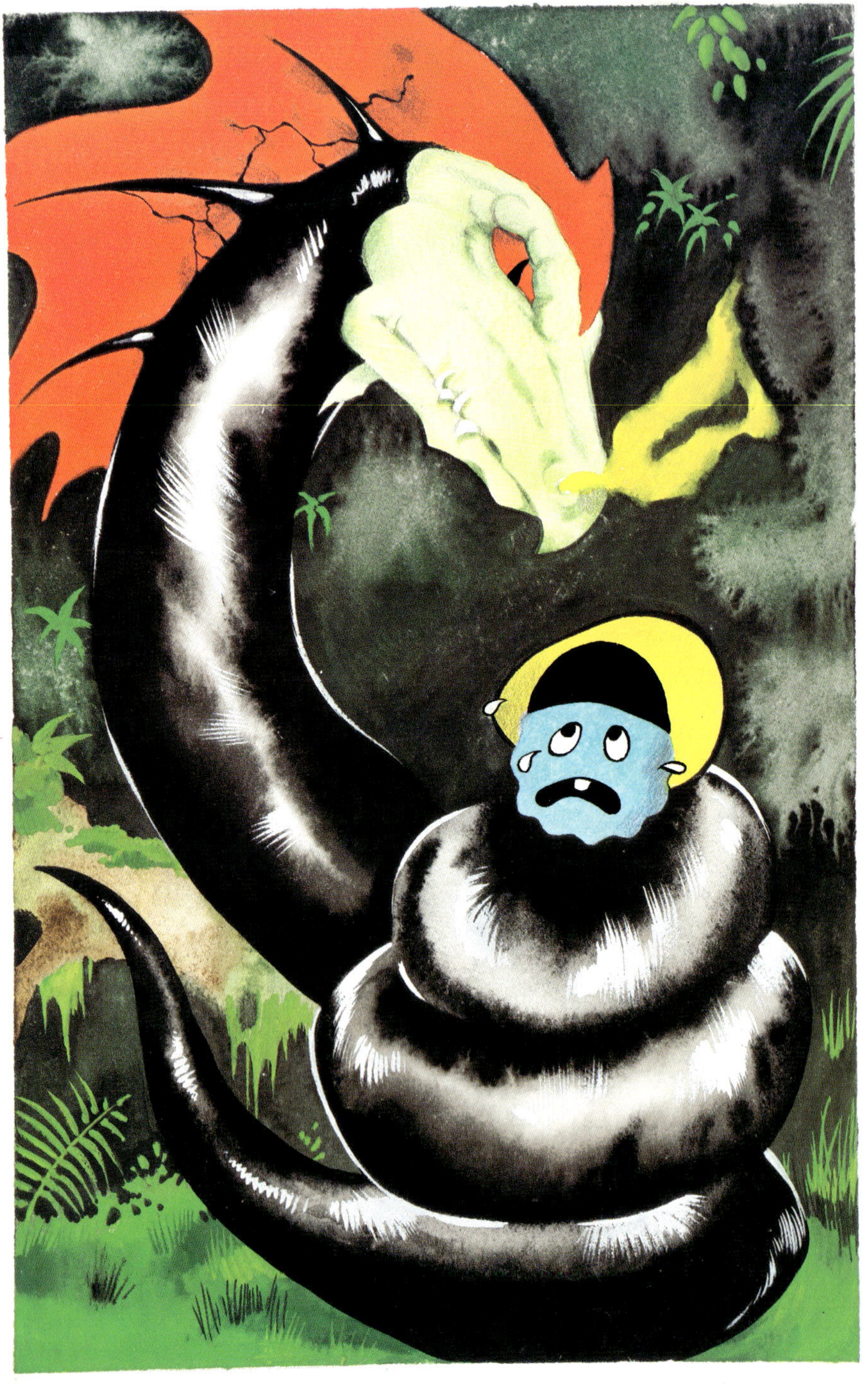

Freddy felt a shudder run up and down his body.
He could not stop himself from shivering.
The wicked snagron began to twist her body around him.
The end of her tail went looping round his legs and feet.
Freddy began to feel dizzy.
He could feel her smooth, slithery skin as she wound herself round his chest and arms.
She felt as slippery as an eel.
By now her head and neck were towering above him.
Her horrid head came zooming down towards him.
Her frowning eyes held him in their spell.
She began to lick her lips greedily.
Little Freddy kept as still as he possibly could.
Would the snagron harm him?
Would she let him live?
Was she hungry?
Would she eat him?

Would she keep him here?
Would she allow him to go free?
Freddy could hardly stand up.
He felt weak and powerless.
The blood was pounding in his chest.
He shut his eyes and began to pray.
Maybe it was all a bad dream!
His body began to sway.
He knew he was going to have a black-out.
Everything went fuzzy and his body went limp, then, 'Stand up!' hissed the snagron. 'Stop slouching about! I need your help.'
The little fuzzbuzz shook his head to get rid of the dizziness, and then he looked up at the snagron.
Somehow, he got his senses back.
'How can I help you?' he asked.
'It's easy!' the snagron said softly.
'Go back to your chief and tell him that I wish to speak to him. Tell him where I am.'
'Yes, yes, I will tell him,' said Freddy.
'Can I set off now?'
'Yes, little one,' hissed the snagron.
'But you must look sharp. Hurry up, and don't be long.'

Freddy was eager to get away.
He ran down the hill as fast as he could.
But when he got to the foot of the hill he stopped.
He looked back towards the snagron.
He stuck his tongue out at her, and then he shouted as loudly as he could.
'You are a big ugly monster. Go back to your glen and stay there, you big bully!'

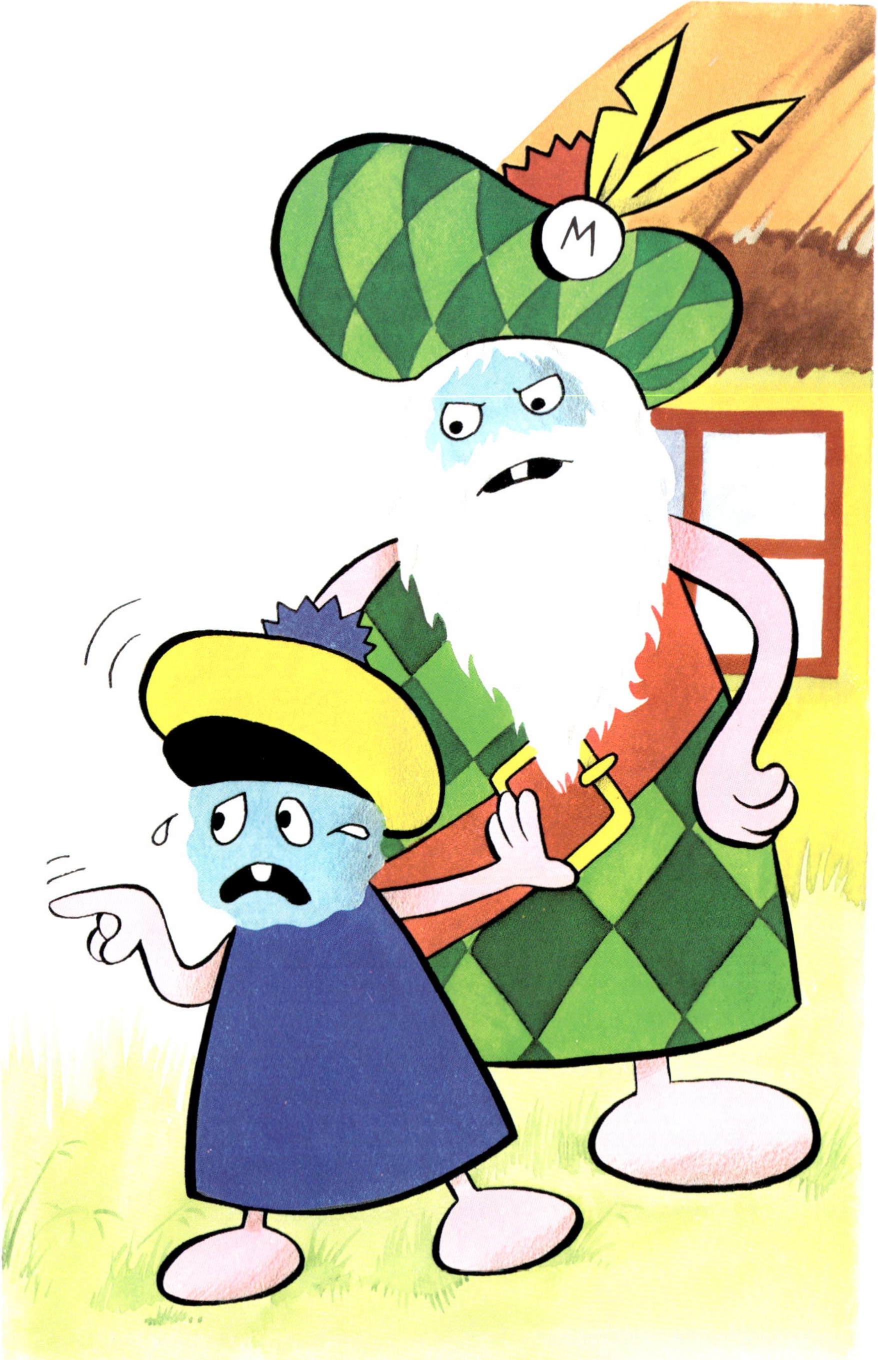

Then little Freddy ran off at top speed.
He ran on and on, not looking where he was going, leaping across rocks and bits of wood. At last, puffing and panting, he made it to the crofts.
'Macfuzz!' he shouted. 'Macfuzz, where are you?'
The chief of the clan came shooting out of his croft.
'What's all the row about?' he asked. 'Why are you shouting so loudly?'
'There's a horrid prowler snooping around in our hills!' said Freddy. 'She said that she is called the snagron. She said that she is the queen of the Glen of Gloom.'
Macfuzz the buzz looked very, very angry.
'What do you think you are saying?' he shouted.
'Are you playing a silly trick on me?'
Then he saw that Freddy was trembling like a leaf.
Macfuzz patted him on the head.
'I'm sorry,' he said. 'I do beg your pardon. Now sit down here and tell me all about it.'

When Freddy had stopped telling the chief about the snagron, Macfuzz the buzz stood up and said, 'Thank goodness that you sounded the alarm.
We must have a meeting. Go and tell everyone to come to my house. Tell them to hurry.'
Little Freddy ran off and the chief began to think of ways of getting rid of the snagron. He knew that this would be a difficult job.
'Well,' he said to himself, 'we will have to deal with her somehow.'
He shook his head sadly and went back into his house.
Before long, all the members of the clan were crowded together on the grass next to the chief's house.
Macfuzz the buzz came out and got up onto a rock so that everybody could see him properly. He put his hands on his hips.
Then he began to speak.
'Something horrid is going to happen,' he said.

27

Everyone started to chatter.

'Now shut up, all of you!' shouted the chief. 'There's a lot I want to say.'

Then he said, 'The thing from the Glen of Gloom is here. She is called the snagron. She is prowling about in the hills and she is probably able to see us now. She says that she wants to meet me.'

'Don't go, don't go!' shouted the clan. 'She's a cheat. She may lay a trap for you. She may kill you!'

Macfuzz the buzz held up his hand.

'Well,' he said, 'I am going to meet her, but I am not going by myself. We will play a trick on her. We will all go. And what's more, we will teach her a lesson she will never forget. Does everyone agree with me?'

'Hooray,' shouted the clan. 'Yes, yes, let's all go!'

'Good,' said Macfuzz. 'Now we must get ready to attack her. There are lots of things we need. Big Ben, you go and get your blunderbuss. Jock, you go with him. The rest of you, go and get anything that will help us. Has anybody got any questions?'

Nobody said a word.

'Smashing,' said Macfuzz. 'I am counting on all of you. Off you go now, and get back here as fast as you can.'

Each member of the clan ran off.

Big Ben lifted his blunderbuss out of its blue box.

Jock put heaps of bullets into his pocket.

Black Angus found a big garden fork.

Tosh found a big steel hammer.

Hilda took the biggest wooden spoon from the rack in her kitchen.

Don found a big wooden club.

It was far too big for him to carry, but he insisted on dragging it along.

At last, all the clan were back, crowding round the chief.

'Splendid!' said Macfuzz, looking around. 'Everyone has found something for the attack.' And pulling out the silver dagger from the sheath on his belt, he said, 'Come on then, let's go! Windbag, you can lead the way.'

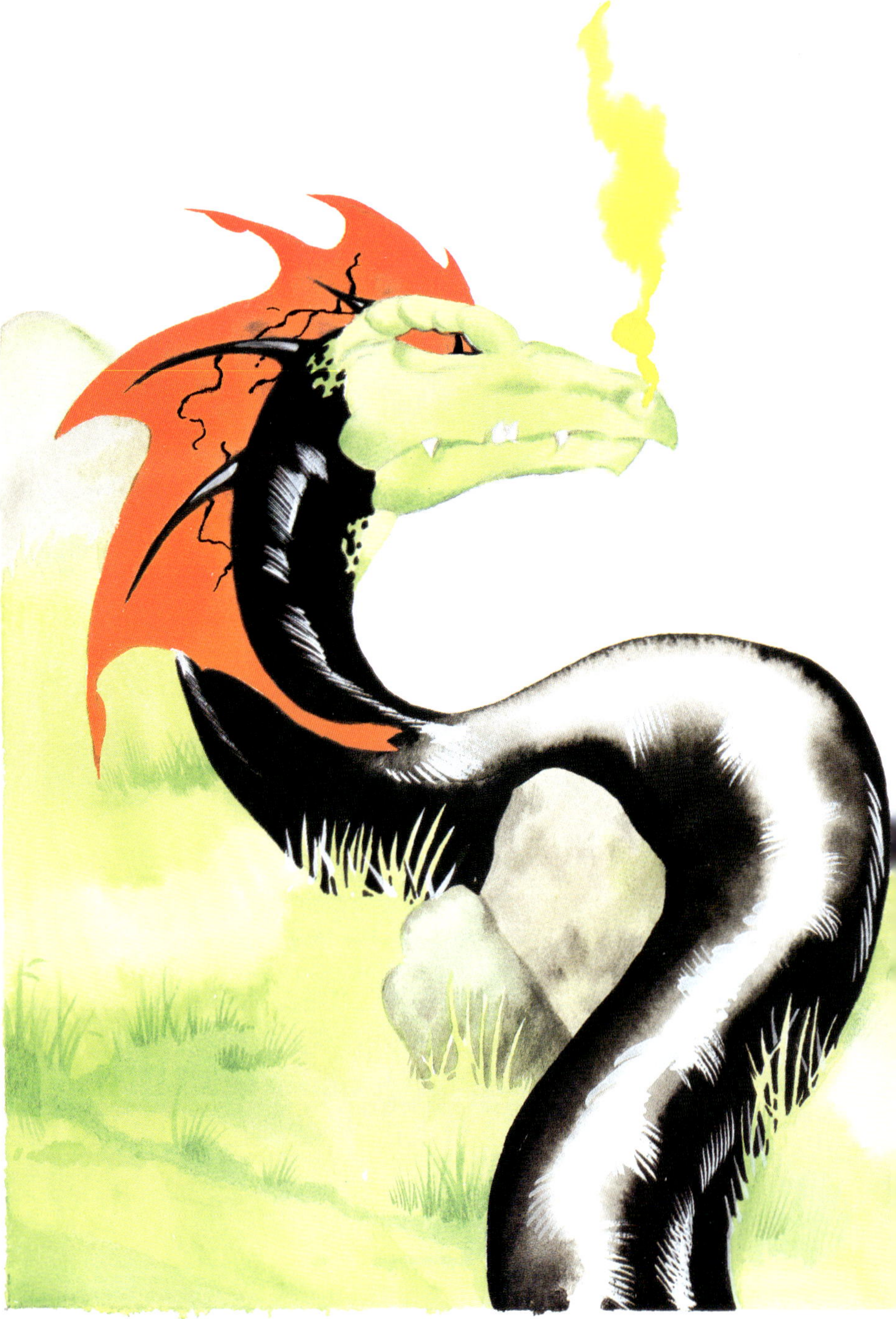

The clan began to march up the hill like a little army.

Windbag went first, playing the bagpipes.

Up on the brow of the hill, the snagron had seen what the clan were up to.

She could see them marching up the hill to attack her.

She began to twist about.

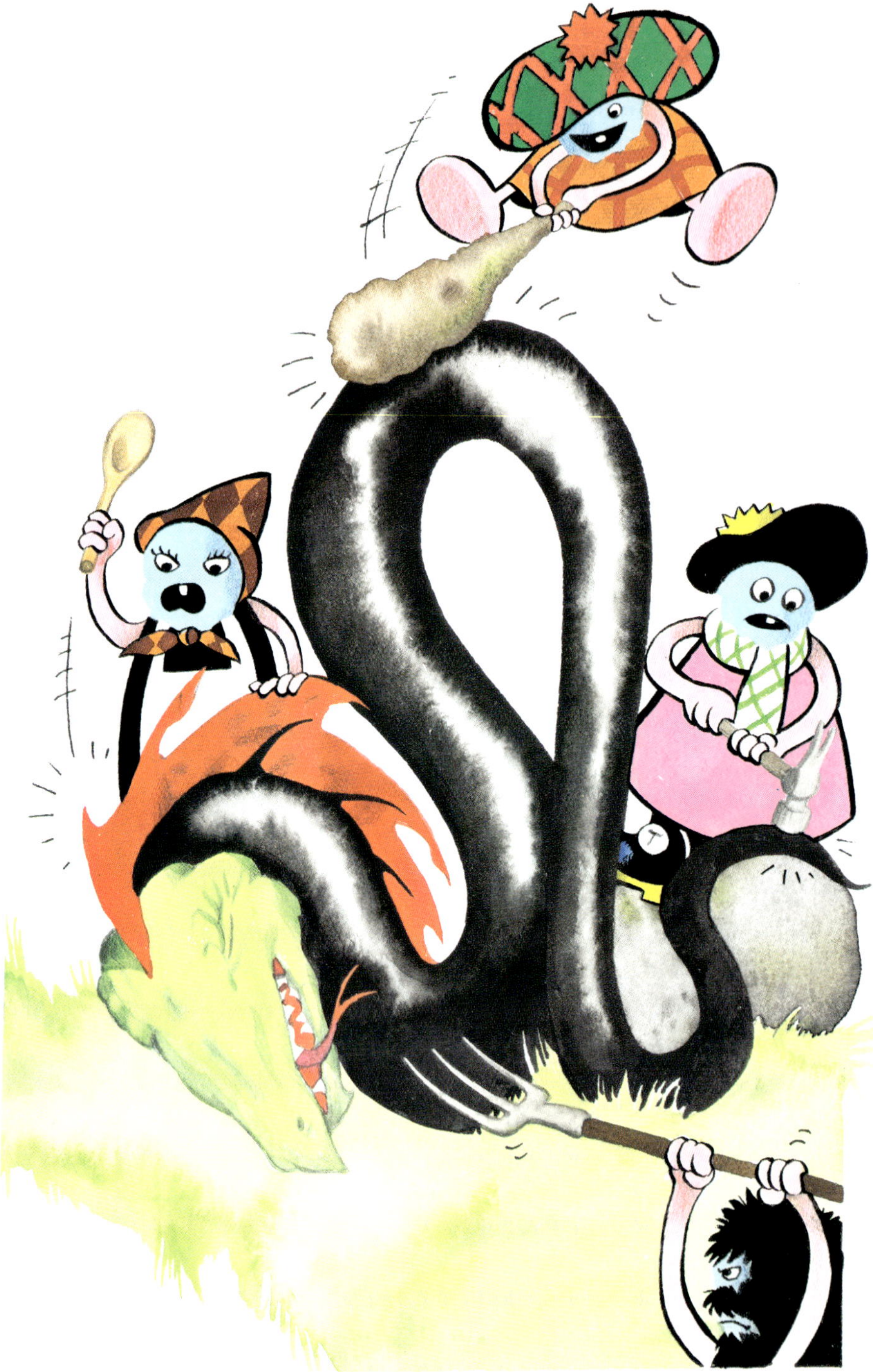

'I'll soon deal with this foolish lot!' she hissed to herself. 'They will be sorry that they ever met me.'
And as the clan came up to the little wood, the snagron slid out to meet them.
'So, so, so,' she hissed. 'I ask to speak to your leader, and you all come to meet me.'
'We have not come to meet you,' shouted Macfuzz the buzz. 'We have come to get rid of you.'
And without giving the snagron a second to think, he shouted, 'Come on, clan Macfuzz. Down with the snagron!'
With a terrific shout, the clan went swooping towards the snagron.
Hilda got there first.
She clouted the snagron on the head with her big wooden spoon.
    POW!
Little Don was battering the snagron's body with his club.
    THUMP!
Tosh pounded the snagron's tail with his hammer.
    CRASH!

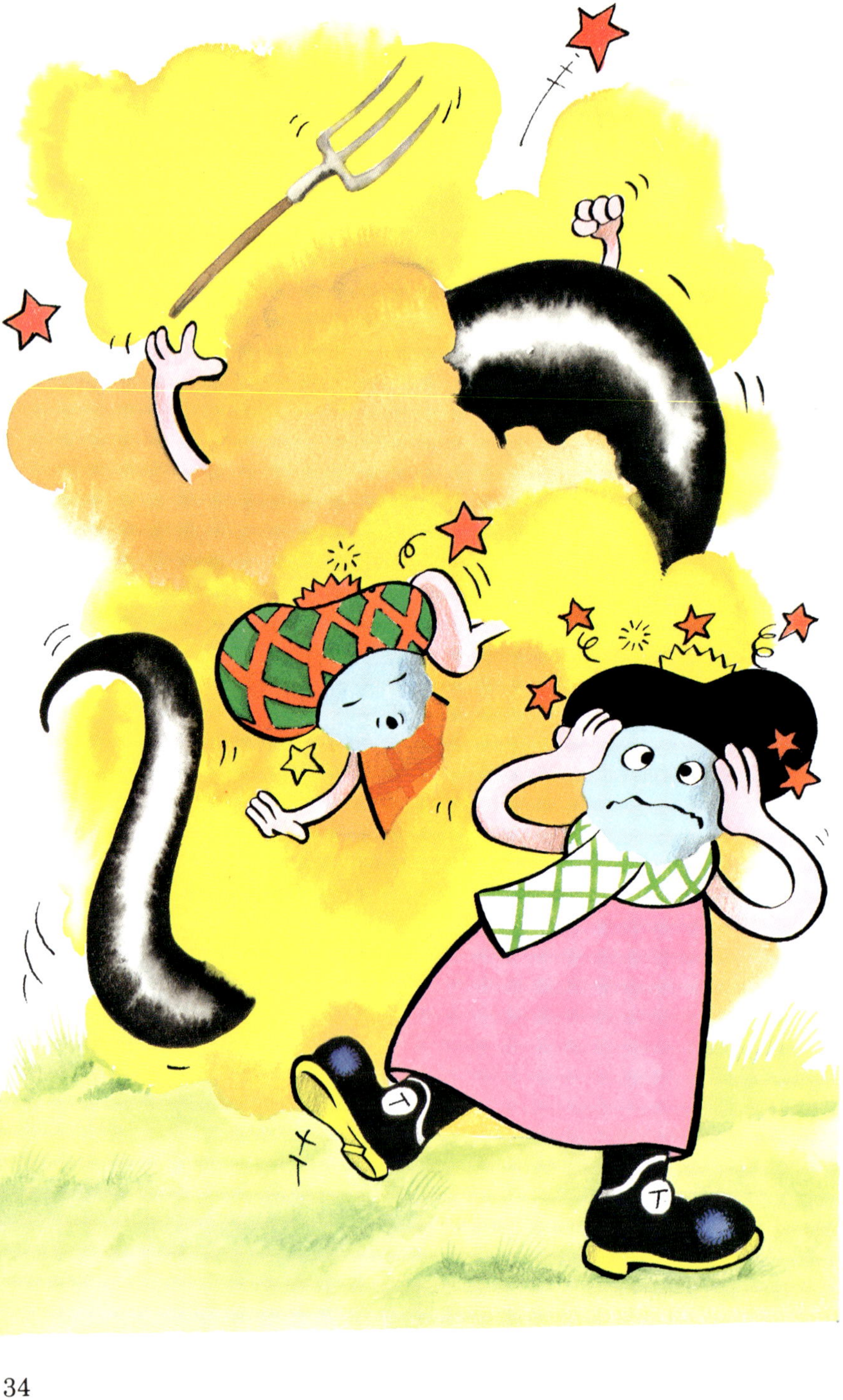

Black Angus was swinging the garden fork round and round his head.

SWISH!

Big Ben was rushing here and there, eagerly looking for a target to shoot at.
But everything was happening far too fast for him to get a good shot in.
Then, little by little, the snagron began to win.
Clouds of powdery dust and yellow mist were getting into the eyes and mouths of the clan. The glen was ringing with the sounds of snarls, howls, screams, and growls.
Every now and then, one of the clan would shout for help as the snagron's teeth found their mark.

ouch! eek! arr! ow! oo! er!

The glen was full of their shouts and screeches.
Tosh came reeling out of the dust and mist. The snagron's tail had hit him so hard that he was seeing stars.
With her eyes sparkling and her teeth snapping, the snagron seemed to be getting bigger and bigger.

Her head seemed to tower above them all.
Her tail was swishing powerfully.
Puffs of thick yellow mist came spouting from her nostrils.
The members of the clan could not see a thing.
One by one, they fell down in a heap.
Soon, just the chief and Windbag were left standing.
It was no good.
The clan was beaten.
'Scatter!' shouted the chief. 'Everyone back to their crofts!'
The clan began to stagger downhill.
Some of them fell down, but they soon got up again.
Panting and gasping, they ran into the first house they came to.
Luckily, they all got in before the snagron could reach them.
Some of the clan started to hide.
Hilda crept underneath a big couch.
Don hid his head under the carpet.
Tosh and Windbag got under the bed.
Macfuzz the buzz put a thick wooden bar across the doorway to shut them all in.

The snagron came slithering up to the door. She was angry with herself for not catching one of the clan, but she was glad that she had beaten them.

'I am the winner! I am the winner!' she hissed, and she sounded as proud as a peacock. 'I beat you all!' she went on. 'You ran away like cowards. I'm so clever! I'm so smart! Nobody can outwit me! You will have to do much better if you want to beat me.

'I can beat any number of you. I bet I could beat a thousand of you. I bet I would be able to beat ten thousand of you! Anyway, I beat you all so easily today.'
'Go away, you big bully!' shouted Macfuzz.
The snagron lifted up her ugly head and looked at the doorway.
'So, Macfuzz the buzz, you think you can get away from me, do you? You fool! You cannot stay in there for ever. Mark my words, it is just a matter of time before I come back again. Then we will see what happens. Yes, indeed we will.'
Then hissing and spitting, the snagron made her way back up into the hills.
The clan hid in the little yellow and brown house for a long, long time.
It was getting dark when at last Macfuzz took the bar down from the door.
The members of the clan crept out into the glen. They all began to ask questions.
'Has she gone away for good?' asked Don.
'She said she would come back again!' said Windbag.

'What will she do next?' asked Hilda.
Nobody could answer her.
Far, far away, a dog began to howl.
They all started to shiver.
As they looked up at the dark, moonless sky, they were all thinking about Hilda's question.
What would the snagron do next?

Now write. Answer all the questions.
Do not forget where to put full stops and capital letters.

1. Where were the little ones playing? (7)
2. What had Hilda made for them to drink? (5)
3. Which member of the clan had not forgotten about the monster? (7)
4. Read these words:
   ferns   rocks   wood
   Now put in the missing word:
   The snagron was hidden by a mound of _____ at the top of the hill. (8)
5. What did Ben play with the little ones? (13)
6. Which little fuzzbuzz ran into the woods? (15)
7. What was Ben's gun called? (29)
8. What part of the snagron did Hilda hit? (33)
9. Where did Little Don hide? (36)
10. Draw the clan attacking the snagron. Draw the monster. Colour it in.